Ladybird FIRST FACTS ABOUT
ANIMALS

By Caroline Arnold
Illustrated by Meryl Henderson

Ladybird Books

Did you know that there are 3 million different kinds of animals in the world?

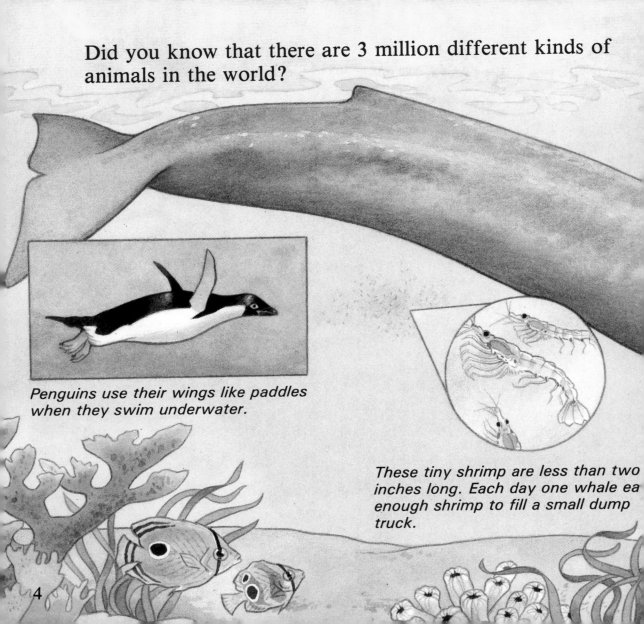

Penguins use their wings like paddles when they swim underwater.

These tiny shrimp are less than two inches long. Each day one whale ea enough shrimp to fill a small dump truck.

4

FIRST FACTS ABOUT...ANIMALS

You can see animals in parks, at the zoo, and even in your own back yard. In this book you will find out about many kinds of animals and what they do. Here are some amazing animal facts:

Tallest animal: A giraffe can be more than 18 feet tall.

Largest land animal: An elephant weighs 6 tons or more.

Smallest mammal: A bumblebee bat weighs less than an ounce.

Fastest animal: A cheetah can run at 70 miles per hour in short spurts.

Slowest mammal: A three-toed sloth moves at about 6-8 feet a minute.

Smallest bird: One kind of hummingbird is only 2 inches long.

Largest bird: An ostrich is 8 feet tall and weighs over 300 pounds.

Longest-living animal: Tortoises have been known to live more than 150 years.

Longest snake: A python can grow up to 30 feet long.

Ladybird First Facts About ™ and its accompanying logo
are registered trademarks of Ladybird Books Ltd.

LADYBIRD BOOKS, INC.
Auburn, Maine 04210 U.S.A.
© LADYBIRD BOOKS LTD 1990
Loughborough, Leicestershire, England

Printed in England

They come in all sizes, shapes, and colors, and you can find them in all kinds of places.

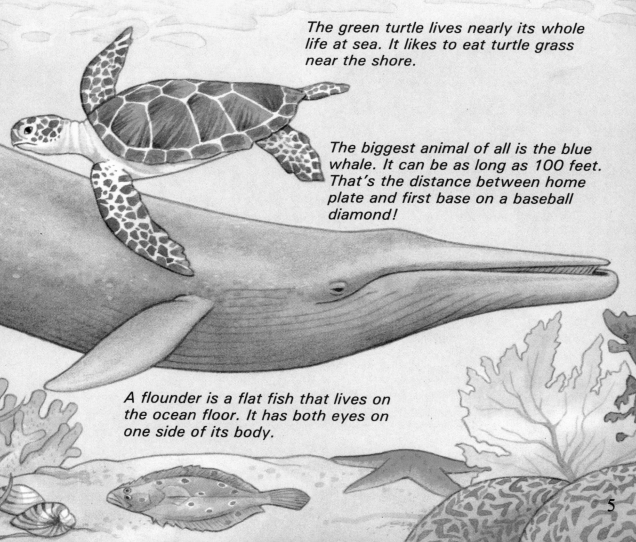

The green turtle lives nearly its whole life at sea. It likes to eat turtle grass near the shore.

The biggest animal of all is the blue whale. It can be as long as 100 feet. That's the distance between home plate and first base on a baseball diamond!

A flounder is a flat fish that lives on the ocean floor. It has both eyes on one side of its body.

All animals belong to one of two groups—those that have backbones and those that do not.

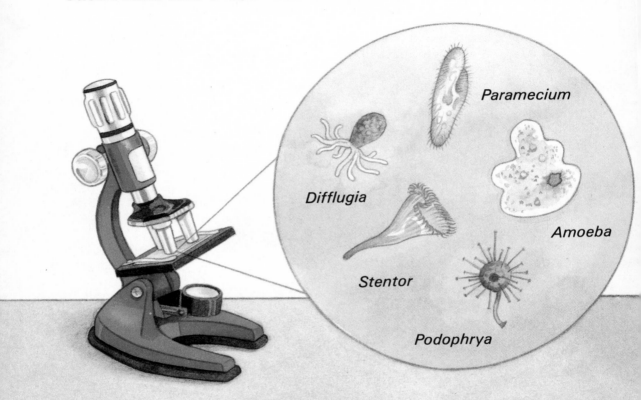

Animals that do not have backbones are called *invertebrates*. The simplest animals belong to this group. Some of them are so small you can see them only through a microscope. These tiny animals often live in pond water.

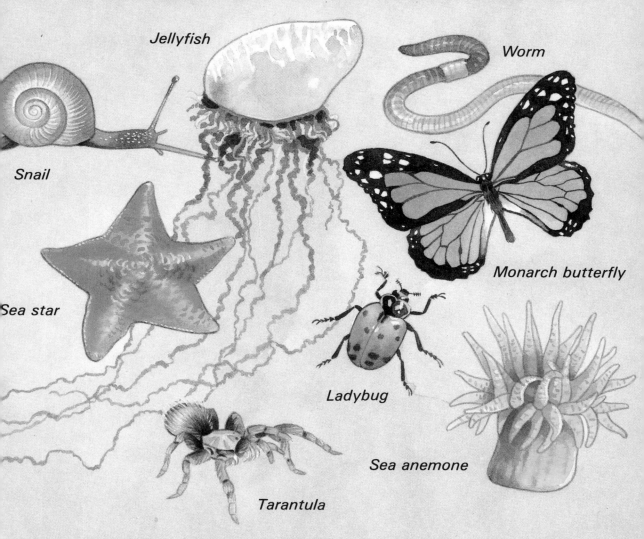

Jellyfish

Worm

Snail

Monarch butterfly

Sea star

Ladybug

Sea anemone

Tarantula

Invertebrates were the first animals to live on earth. These are some of the invertebrates that live on earth today.

Animals with backbones are called *vertebrates*. Mammals, birds, fish, reptiles, and amphibians belong to this group.

Mammals are animals that have fur or hair and feed their babies milk. Human beings are mammals.

Bats are the only mammals that can fly.

Thick fur keeps this raccoon family warm in winter.

This mother pig can feed many babies at the same time.

Birds are animals with feathers. All birds lay eggs, and most of them can fly.

The hummingbird's wings move so fast you cannot see them.

A red-tailed hawk soars on wide wings.

The female robin lays pale blue eggs.

The condor is the largest bird in North America. It is nearly extinct.

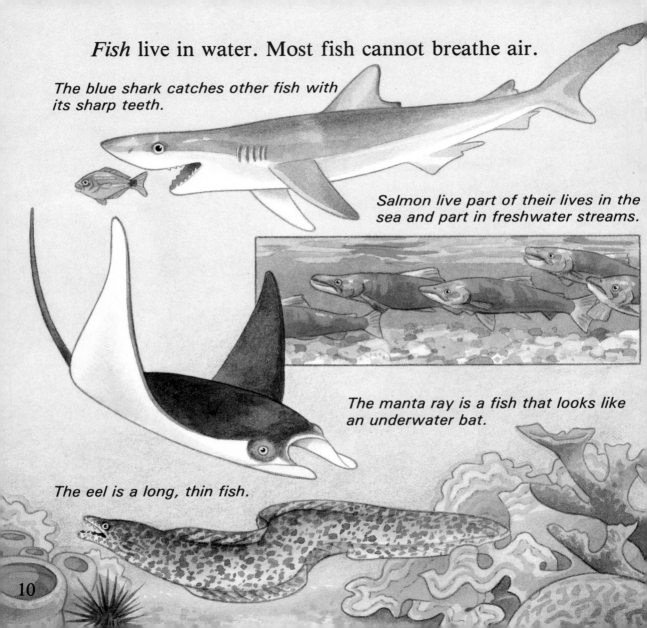

Fish live in water. Most fish cannot breathe air.

The blue shark catches other fish with its sharp teeth.

Salmon live part of their lives in the sea and part in freshwater streams.

The manta ray is a fish that looks like an underwater bat.

The eel is a long, thin fish.

Most *reptiles* have dry, scaly skin. Lizards, snakes, crocodiles, and turtles are reptiles.

A chameleon can change color to blend into its surroundings.

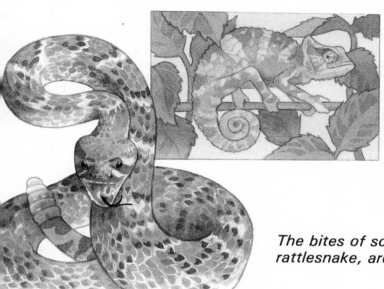

The bites of some snakes, like this rattlesnake, are poisonous.

Amphibians can live both in water and on dry land. Frogs, toads, newts, and salamanders are amphibians.

A frog begins life as a tadpole in the water. As it grows it begins to breathe air.

You can find animals almost everyplace on earth.

Some live in the air.

Bats and most birds and insects can fly.

Some live on land.

Horses, dogs, and ostriches are all good runners.

Some live in the water.

Fish, dolphins, and ducks can swim.

And some live underground.

Moles and worms make tunnels in the earth.

13

Most animals live best in one kind of place.

Some live where it is hot.

Camels and lizards can live in the desert.

Some live where it is cold.

Polar bears and seals live in the Arctic.

Some live high in the mountains.

Mountain goats and eagles like high, rocky ledges.

And some live deep in the forest.

Deer and chipmunks like to live where there are trees.

15

All animals must eat. Food gives them energy to grow and live.

Some animals eat plants.

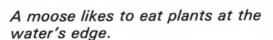

A moose likes to eat plants at the water's edge.

A squirrel collects nuts to store for the winter.

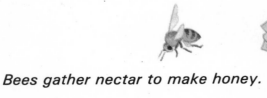

Bees gather nectar to make honey.

Some animals eat meat.

This fox is hunting for rabbits and other small animals.

A great blue heron searches for fish in the shallow water.

Some animals eat both plants and meat.

Bears eat leaves and berries, but they also like fish.

17

Most animals are able to move, so they can find food and shelter.

Some walk, run, or hop.

A kangaroo can hop more than 40 feet in one leap!

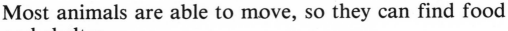

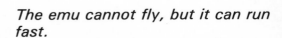

The emu cannot fly, but it can run fast.

Some climb.

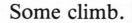

A koala spends most of its life high in the treetops.

Some wriggle or slide.

The amethystine python is the longest snake in Australia. It can be 24 feet long.

Some swim.

A duck-billed platypus has web-shaped feet that are good for swimming. It is one of only two mammals that lay eggs.

...nd some fly.

...cks of cockatoos search for fruit to ...t.

19

Every animal must be able to protect itself from danger. Some fight, some hide, and some run away.

A herd of zebra runs away. The animals sense that an enemy is near.

A lion fights with sharp teeth and claws.

When a young gazelle lies still in the tall grass it is hard to see.

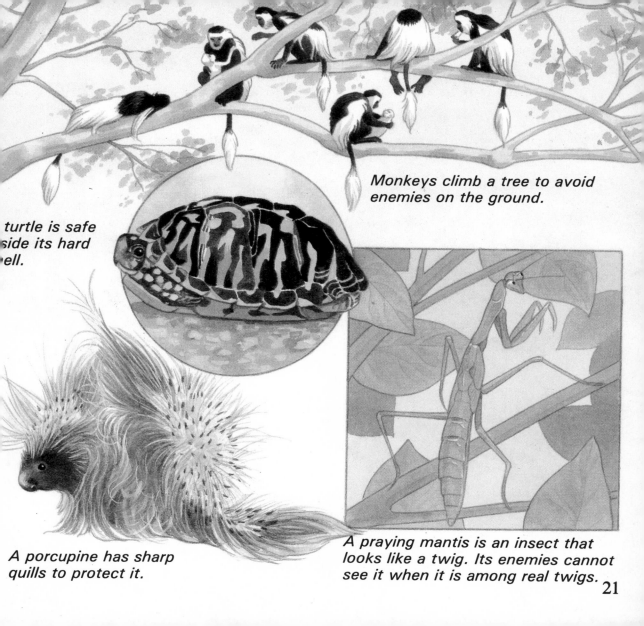

Monkeys climb a tree to avoid enemies on the ground.

turtle is safe
side its hard
ell.

A porcupine has sharp quills to protect it.

A praying mantis is an insect that looks like a twig. Its enemies cannot see it when it is among real twigs.

21

Most animals mate and have young.

Some animals have just one or a few babies at a time.

A pair of bluejays often have four hungry babies to feed.

A mother chimpanzee usually takes care of her single baby for several years.

A mother deer often has twins.

And some animals produce many offspring all at once.

A female turtle may lay up to 100 eggs in her nest.

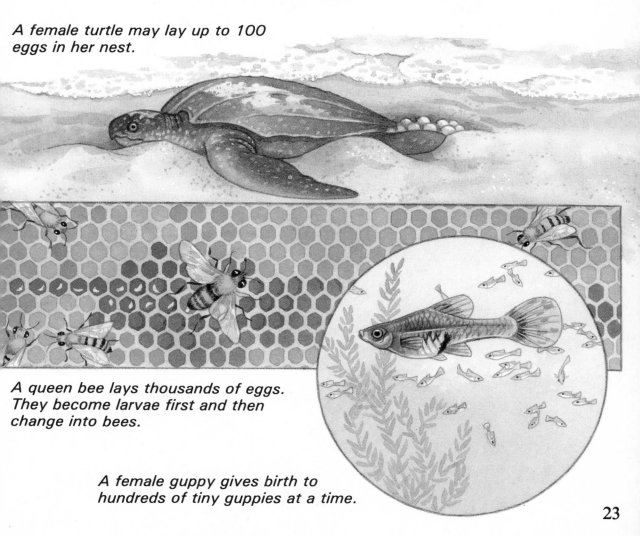

A queen bee lays thousands of eggs. They become larvae first and then change into bees.

A female guppy gives birth to hundreds of tiny guppies at a time.

23

Animals cannot talk like people do. But they communicate in other ways.

Sometimes they make noises.

A male sparrow sings to defend his nest and attract a mate.

A cat hisses to warn another animal to stay away.

A moose bull bellows to challenge other bulls.

Sometimes they use body signals.

A dog wags its tail as a greeting.

A peacock raises his tail feathers to impress the peahen.

Sometimes they communicate in other ways.

Ants leave a scent trail to tell other ants where to find food.

Fireflies blink their lights to show one another where they are.

25

Each kind of animal is special in its own way. Its shape, size, and color help it to do what it needs to live.

The elephant's trunk can be used like a hose when it wants to cool off.

The giraffe's long neck helps it reach leaves to eat on tall trees.

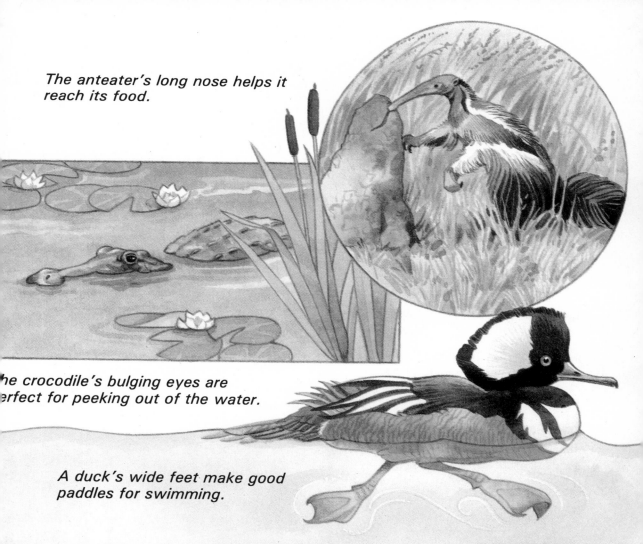

The anteater's long nose helps it reach its food.

The crocodile's bulging eyes are perfect for peeking out of the water.

A duck's wide feet make good paddles for swimming.

No two animals are alike. Each one is part of the amazing world we live in.

27

GLOSSARY

amphibian   an animal that can live both in water and on land

Arctic   the region of the North Pole

bird   a two-footed animal with feathers and wings

communicate   to give or exchange information

extinct   no longer existing; a kind of animal or plant that once existed on earth and is now completely gone is *extinct*

fish   an animal that lives entirely in the water and breathes through gills

invertebrates   animals that do not have backbones

mammals   animals with fur or hair that feed their babies milk

reptiles   animals such as lizards and snakes, with scaly, dry skin

scent trail   trail made by depositing small amounts of strong-smelling substances on the ground

vertebrates   animals that have backbones